THE LEGEND OF ATLANTIS

by Thomas Kingsley Troupe

illustrated by Mike Cressy

PICTURE WINDOW BOOKS
a capstone imprint

Thanks to our advisers for their expertise, research, and advice:

Elizabeth Tucker, Professor of English
Binghamton University
Binghamton, New York

Terry Flaherty, PhD, Professor of English
Minnesota State University, Mankato

Editor: Shelly Lyons
Designer: Heidi Thompson
Art Director: Nathan Gassman
Production Specialist: Danielle Ceminsky
The illustrations in this book were created digitally.

Picture Window Books
1710 Roe Crest Drive
North Mankato, MN 56003
www.capstonepub.com

All books published by Picture Window Books
are manufactured with paper containing at least
10 percent post-consumer waste.

Library of Congress Cataloging-in-Publication Data
Troupe, Thomas Kingsley.
  The legend of Atlantis / by Thomas Kingsley Troupe ;
illustrated by Michael Cressy.
    p. cm. — (Legend has it)
  Includes index.
  ISBN 978-1-4048-6656-0 (library binding)
  1. Atlantis (Legendary place)—Juvenile literature. I. Cressy, Mike,
ill. II. Title.
    GN751.T765 2012
      398.23'4—dc23
                                            2011025838

Printed in the United States of America in North Mankato, Minnesota.
102011   006405CGS12

TABLE of CONTENTS

LOST CITY OF THE SEA

Somewhere in the ocean lies a legendary city. Statues of silver and gold stand inside a beautiful temple. This is a kingdom fit for the gods. Welcome to the lost city of Atlantis!

The city of Atlantis rested on an island of the same name. Thousands of years ago, all of Atlantis sank to the bottom of the ocean.

ANCIENT WRITINGS

The story of Atlantis is one of the oldest legends. In 355 BC the great Greek philosopher Plato wrote about the island. His texts are the oldest writings about Atlantis.

In one text, he explains that the people of Athens were at war with the people of Atlantis.

Plato also describes the city of Atlantis
in great detail. It was round, with many
canals circling the island.

The land in Atlantis was filled with silver, gold, and a rare precious metal called orichalcum. With orichalcum, the people built monuments. In the middle of the city stood the Temple of Poseidon, built for the Greek god of the sea.

RICH AND POWERFUL PEOPLE

The people of Atlantis were wealthy. They were skilled builders too. Proof could be seen in their magnificent city. Their large homes were made of white, black, and red stone.

The Atlanteans also grew fruits and vegetables the world had never seen. Some say the seedless banana first came from Atlantis!

The legend says after many years, the people of Atlantis began fighting each other.

They no longer felt grateful for what they had.

Their greed upset the gods. Angered, the Greek god Zeus decided to teach the Atlanteans a lesson.

FALL OF ATLANTIS

Soon a great earthquake rumbled, shaking the island. Buildings toppled as the people ran for safety. But there was nowhere to go.

Great waves rose up from the ocean. Seawater crashed across the land and flooded the beautiful city. Quickly, the ocean swallowed up Atlantis.

LOCATION of ATLANTIS

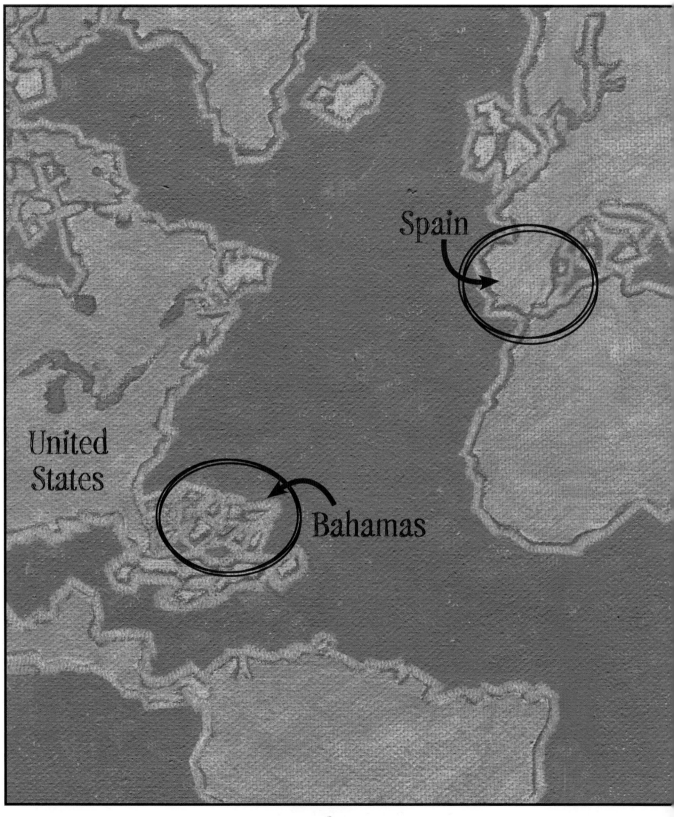

Europe

Africa

No one knows for sure where the city of Atlantis was. Some think Atlantis could have been near the Bahamas or Spain.

Many old maps show a mass of land off the northwest coast of Africa. Could this be where Atlantis once was?

Recently, some people have said the frozen continent of Antarctica might have been Atlantis.

Antarctica

SEARCHING FOR ATLANTIS

Although no one has found a trace of the sunken city, some people still believe Atlantis was real. For hundreds of years, explorers have searched the oceans for clues.

Jacques Collina-Girard,
a French scientist, believes
Atlantis was near the Strait
of Gibraltar. Spartel Island is
there now, but it was flooded
11,000 years ago.

Europe

Strait of Gibraltar

Africa

That's almost exactly
the same time Atlantis
had disappeared,
according to Plato.

In 2004 scientist Rainer Kuehne looked at a satellite image of southern Spain. In a spot called Doñana National Park, he saw unnatural circular shapes on the ground. He even noticed a rectangular shape in the photo. Could it have been Atlantis' Temple of Poseidon?

Spain

Doñana National Park

In 2009 researchers studied the Doñana National Park site. They found two small statues in the dirt. Could these have come from Atlantis?

Experts are still digging at the site.

OTHER LOST CITIES

Atlantis isn't the only mythical place to have vanished. In 1926 Colonel James Churchward explained what he had read on old tablets from India and Mexico.

One text mentioned an island in the Pacific Ocean called Mu. It said that thousands of years ago, Mu sank into the sea when gas caves beneath it exploded.

According to another legend, a wounded
King Arthur went to the Isle of Avalon to die.
But there is no Isle of Avalon now.

In 1191 three monks found what was thought to be Arthur's body in Glastonbury, England. Is it possible that the town of Glastonbury was once the Isle of Avalon?

Though it's still unknown if Atlantis was real, many people wonder about the legend. Could the sea really have swallowed a whole island and beautiful city? Could some of the people have escaped the sinking and settled in other places?

Only the ocean knows for sure.

GLOSSARY

canal—a channel dug across land; canals connect bodies of water so that ships can travel between them

greed—wanting more of something than is actually needed

legend—a story passed down from earlier times that could seem believable

monument—a statue or building that is meant to remind people of an event or person

philosopher—a person who studies truth and knowledge

temple—a building used for worship

READ MORE

Martin, Michael. *Atlantis.* The Unexplained. Mankato, Minn.: Capstone Press, 2007.

Roberts, Russell. *The Lost Continent of Atlantis.* A Robbie Reader. Natural Disasters. Hockessin, Del.: M. Lane Publishers, 2007.

Walker, Kathryn, based on original text by Brian Innes. *The Mystery of Atlantis.* Unsolved! New York: Crabtree Pub. Co., 2010.

INTERNET SITES

FactHound offers a safe, fun way to find Internet sites related to this book. All of the sites on FactHound have been researched by our staff.

Here's all you do:

Visit *www.facthound.com*

Type in this code: 9781404866560

 Check out projects, games and lots more at
www.capstonekids.com

INDEX

THE LEGEND OF ATLANTIS
by Thomas Kingsley Troupe · Illustrated by Mike Chiappa

THE LEGEND OF BIGFOOT
by Thomas Kingsley Troupe · illustrated by Brian Caleb Dumm

THE LEGEND OF THE BERMUDA TRIANGLE
by Thomas Kingsley Troupe · Illustrated by Carlos Aon

The Legend of the LOCH NESS MONSTER
by THOMAS KINGSLEY TROUPE · illustrated by DC ICE

Look for all the books in the
LEGEND HAS IT
series

THE LEGEND OF UFOs

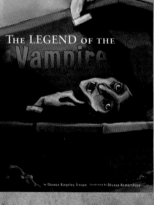

THE LEGEND OF THE Vampire
by Thomas Kingsley Troupe · illustrated by Oksana Kemarskaya

The Legend of the Werewolf
BY THOMAS KINGSLEY TROUPE · ILLUSTRATED BY DC ICE

written by THOMAS KINGSLEY TROUPE · illustrated by FRANCESCA ROSSI VIGIBALA

THE LEGEND OF THE

Friends of the
Houston Public Library